P9-AOA-574

This Very Merry Christmas Keepbook
Belongs to

Stacé

Who Live in *aspen*

Date *Dec 82*

A Merry Christmas

AN OLD FASHIONED KEEPBOOK™

Our Christmas Book

By Linda Campbell Franklin

Designed by Sara Bowman

Tree Communications, Inc.

New York City

© 1981, Tree Communications, Inc.
All rights reserved. No part of this work may be
reproduced or transmitted in any form by any
means, electronic or mechanical, including
photocopying and recording, or by any
information storage or retrieval system without
permission in writing from the publisher.

Published in the United States by
Tree Communications, Inc.,
250 Park Avenue South,
New York, New York, 10003
Printed in the United States of America

Cover fabric design © 1977 VIP Fabrics
Division, Cranston Print Works Company

ISBN 0-934504-09-1
Library of Congress Catalog Card No. 81–52491

This book was typeset in Goudy Old Style by
David E. Seham Associates, Inc. Color
separations were made by Daiichi Seihan Co.
The paper is 70 lb Warren Olde Style, cream,
supplied by Baldwin Paper Company. The book
was printed and bound by R. R. Donnelley &
Sons Company.

Write us about other books in the Keepbook series.

A very Merry Christmas to all the people who have contributed their time and talents to the creation of Our Christmas Book! Special thanks go to Michael Gross, Mary Mac Franklin and Robert D. Franklin for research and for their stories and prayer. I am also grateful for the cooperation of Phillip Snyder who collects Christmas tree ornaments and Earl W. Kage who collects manger scenes. I acknowledge my thanks to Sheila Clemett for her eyesight and her help. Congratulations to Sara Bowman for her design of this book, and to her assistants Rosie Mackiewicz and Carolyn Ogden. Noël to Rene Aussoleil for his help. Thanks to Martha Lipton for her drawings. Our Christmas Book is dedicated with love from all of us at Tree Communications to all of you.

Dear Friends,

Christmas is such a special time. More than ever we know how precious are friends and family, and how deep are our sentiments. It is a season of rebirth and reunion; a time to relive traditions which our families have shared for dozens of years; a time to welcome new members to the family fold.

With great pleasure we present to you Our Christmas Book, and by means of it share the holiday with you.

Best Wishes!

Linda Campbell Franklin

Table of Contents

Songs & Music

 # A Small Christmas Miracle

Christmas Eve day was a busy time at the McRee's. Mummy, Daddy, Sam and Katy decorated their house. They decorated it all over: the porch columns were wrapped with evergreens, Katy hung ornaments on the leafless climbing roses, and even the gate opening into their yard got a beribboned swag of balsam and boxwood. Dried pine cones, fastened on with bread-wrapper twists, danced and bobbed when the gate was opened. Daddy made the outside door wreath of evergreens, and Mummy hung a calico wreath on the inside of the kitchen door.

The entrance hall looked the best it ever had. Katy made a wreath to fit around the big mirror. She used sprigs of holly, evergreens, popcorn and cranberries. Then she tucked in ivy to fill the gaps, and tied on tiny satin ribbons and Christmas bows from all their Christmases past.

Below the wreath, on top of a low chest, Sam laid a bed of small pine tree branches. He arranged on it a tin whistle, a golden plastic horn, a toy drum he had had when he was a *little* boy (he was nine this year), and a very pretty silver harp that had belonged to his grandmother and was really a pin. Katy let Sam hang his shiny triangle, left over from nursery school, from the bottom of her wreath.

On Christmas Eve night, the McRees had a wonderful party. The Marchionis (all six of them, because this year nobody had croup) were there. The Wilsons came. They had just moved in across the street and were happy to be welcomed to the neighborhood at a holiday celebration. All the Bancrofts from up the road and the Fullers from down the hill came too. Just as Sam—who was more than ready—wailed "Suppose nobody at all comes to our party?" everyone arrived at once. They came in laughing and calling out "Merry Christmas!" and they admired the three wreaths and the tiny orchestra of toy instruments.

First they sang all the old familiar carols. Then they tried out some new songs that made them giggle because no-one sang in the right key, and never finished at the same time. The children stood in front of the fireplace and sang *Away in a Manger* for their parents. The women stood around the piano and sang *God Rest Ye Merry, Gentlemen,* and then the men sang *We Three Kings of Orient Are,* even though there were five of them.

The Christmas cookies lasted all through the party, and the *Kugelkachen* did too, and the cranberry juice and ginger ale punch almost lasted, but not quite. The singers all had parched throats by eight-thirty, and the party wasn't over until nine o'clock.

Just as the neighbors stood up to go, the sounds of *Silent Night, Holy Night* floated in from the hall. A harp solo, a tinkling triangle, then the drum started in, and they could hear *Away in a Manger.* Everyone crept quietly toward the arch which led to the hall. The arrangement on the chest beneath the mirror was shining in the soft light. The instruments, that Sam had laid so carefully in the pine needles, were playing carols for their family.

Suddenly the notes became louder, and the instruments were playing exultant, joyous music that filled the hall. The grown-ups turned to each other and cried *"The Hallelujuh Chorus!"* How could tin and silver and plastic and a little dimestore drum play the magnificent *Hallelujah?* They all knew, as they put their arms around each other, that what Sam whispered is true: "Christmas *is* a miracle!"   Mary Mac Franklin

Joy to the World

Joy to the world! the Lord is come; Let earth re- ceive her King; Let

ev- 'ry heart pre- pare Him room, And heav'n and na- ture

sing, And heav'n and na- ture sing, And heav'n and heav'n and na- ture sing.

Joy to the earth! the Savior reigns;
Let men their songs employ;
While fields and floods, rocks, hills and plains,
Repeat the sounding joy.

No more let sins and sorrows grow,
Nor thorns infest the ground;
He comes to make His blessings flow
Far as the curse is found.

He rules the world with truth and grace;
And makes the nations prove
The glories of His righteousness,
And wonders of His Love.

*Hymn by Isaac Watts, 1719, newly set to music in
the 19th century by Dr. Lowell Mason*

Away in a Manger

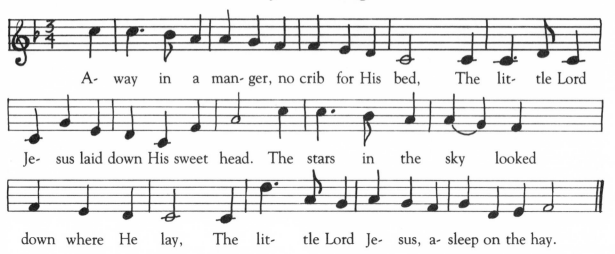

A-way in a man-ger, no crib for His bed, The lit-tle Lord Je-sus laid down His sweet head. The stars in the sky looked down where He lay, The lit-tle Lord Je-sus, a-sleep on the hay.

The cattle are lowing, the poor Baby wakes,
But little Lord Jesus, no crying He makes.
I love Thee, Lord Jesus, look down from the sky,
And stay by my cradle till morning is nigh.

Be near me, Lord Jesus, I ask Thee to stay
Close by me forever and love me, I pray;
Bless all the dear children in Thy tender care,
And take us to heaven, to live with Thee there.

*Words are from an anonymous Lutheran hymnal from
1885. The tune which we sing now dates from 1887.*

Silent Night

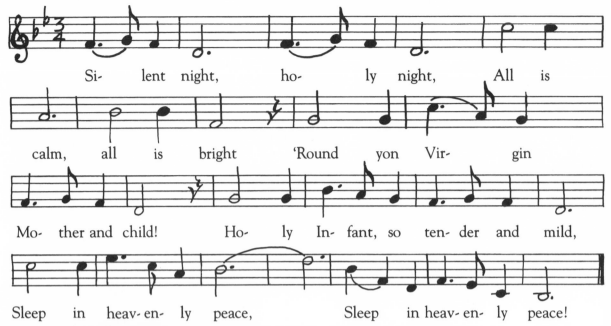

Si- lent night, ho- ly night, All is
calm, all is bright 'Round yon Vir- gin
Mo- ther and child! Ho- ly In- fant, so ten- der and mild,
Sleep in heav- en- ly peace, Sleep in heav- en- ly peace!

Silent night, holy night,
Shepherds quake at the sight,
Glories stream from heaven afar,
Heavenly hosts sing alleluia;
Christ, the Saviour, is born!

Silent night, holy night,
Son of God, love's pure light
Radiant beams from Thy holy face,
With the dawn of redeeming grace,
Jesus, Lord, at Thy birth!

*Words by Joseph Mohr and music by Franz Zavier Grüber, 1819
English translation by Reverend John Freeman Young, 1863.*

Deck the Halls with Boughs of Holly

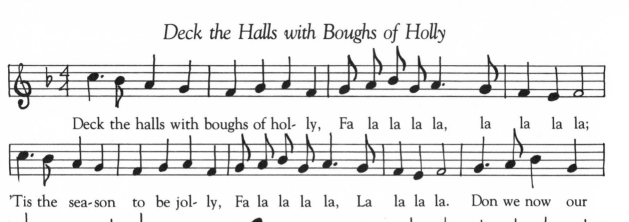

Deck the halls with boughs of hol- ly, Fa la la la la, la la la la;

'Tis the sea-son to be jol- ly, Fa la la la la, La la la la. Don we now our

gay ap-par- el, Fa la la, fa la la, la la la; Troll the an- cient Yule- tide car- ol,

Fa la la la la, la la la la!

See the blazing yule before us,
Fa la la la la, la la la la;
Strike the harp and join the chorus,
Fa la la la la, la la la la.
Follow me in merry measure,
Fa la la, fa la la, la la la,
While I tell of Christmas treasure,
Fa la la la la, la la la la!

Fast away the old year passes,
Fa la la la la, la la la la;
Hail the new, ye lads and lasses,
Fa la la la la, la la la la.
Sing we joyous songs together,
Fa la la, fa la la, la la la,
Heedless of the wind and weather,
Fa la la la la, la la la la!

*This secular carol is anonymous and probably Welsh.
It was known in the 18th century, but may have been
written in the 17th.*

Foods
& Feasts

A Caroling Party:
BEFORE & AFTER

ho can resist going to the window or door on a wintry night to watch for the arrival of a group of carolers whose voices announce their joyful progress along the street where you live? This year, whether you join such a group, or stay snug at home enjoying the songs, you can plan a very simple party.

If you and your family or friends will be going out to sing in your neighborhood, plan to serve something warming and tasty beforehand. This is a good time for hot mulled cider, spicy with cinnamon and cloves, and a few crisp ginger cookies such as those on page 18. For the same reason that opera singers won't drink milk before a performance, carolers will find that their throats are clearer if they save the hot chocolate until the evening's end. If you stay at home, invite carolers in for a few minutes' warmth and rest and share cider and cookies with them. You can mix up a quicker batch of cider by adding ¼ teaspoon ground cloves and ½ teaspoon cinnamon, boiling and serving immediately, after straining.

HOT MULLED CIDER FOR TEN

Mix 2 quarts of apple cider, ¼ cup of brown sugar, 12 whole cloves, ¼ teaspoon allspice, 1 teaspoon ground cinnamon, and a dash of salt in a heavy saucepan. Bring to a boil, stirring constantly, then turn back the heat and simmer for five minutes. Cool, cover, and refrigerate. Shortly before serving, strain to remove cloves, then reheat. Serve in heated mugs with a very thin slice of lemon (rind and all) and a cinnamon stick stirrer.

HEART-WARMING MOCHA FOR TEN

In a large double boiler, mix a scant ½ cup of sugar, ½ cup unsweetened cocoa, 3 tablespoons of instant coffee (decaffeinated or regular), ½ teaspoon cinnamon and ⅛ teaspoon salt. Warm 1½ cups milk and mix into dry ingredients with an eggbeater until creamy and smooth. Add another 6½ cups milk and heat. Do not allow to scald. With eggbeater, mix in ¾ teaspoon vanilla extract. Serve in hot mugs with whipped cream or marshmallow topping, if desired.

Caroling-along

We, the undersigned, joined a caroling party:

We sang the following carols:

We went out on the night of _____.

The temperature was _____ °F.

The weather was _____

_____

Our route went like this: _____

_____

_____

The leader, or pitchpipe, of our group was _____.

_____

The best thing about the party was _____

_____ and the

worst thing was _____

_____

_____!

Moravian Ginger Cookies

Yields: about 50 cookies

8 cups all-purpose flour
1 tablespoon ground cloves
1 tablespoon ground cinnamon
1-½ teaspoons ground ginger
1-¾ cups brown sugar
2 cups shortening (unsalted butter and lard)
½ teaspoon baking soda, dissolved in
1 teaspoon cider vinegar
4 cups unsulphered molasses or dark corn syrup

Cookie sheets, fancy cookie cutters

n a very large mixing bowl, sift the flour and spices together. Mix in the sugar. With a pastry blender or your fingers, work the shortening into the dry mixture. When the dough is crumbly, add the baking soda/vinegar mixture and the molasses. Mix very thoroughly. Divide into balls about the size of a baseball. Chill the balls in the refrigerator for at least an hour. [*Preheat oven to 350°F.*] Roll very thin. Cut into stars, bells, hearts, Santas, reindeer, wreaths, etc. Or make paper templates from cardboard of little boys and girls, and cut around the template with a table knife. Or draw around each child's hand on cardboard, cut out, and use these hand shapes as templates for more cookies. If you plan to hang the cookies on the tree, make a ½″ hole in an appropriate place in each cookie. The hand-shaped cookies can be made to hang by gently joining the thumb and forefinger. Put the cookies on an ungreased cookie sheet—far enough apart so that if the cookies spread a bit during baking they won't touch each other. Bake for about 10 to 12 minutes. Cool on racks. These are very crisp cookies and should be stored loosely covered rather than in an airtight tin.

'Twas Two Nights Before Christmas

Santa is in his workshop at the North Pole. It is December 23, and he is suffering a bout of pre-Christmas nerves. The elves are gathered around his feet as he thumbs through his portrait album, viewing with some disdain various images of him that have come down through the centuries. He speaks:

"This air-of-mystery business is all well and good, but look what it has gotten me—all these distortions and misrepresentations of my appearance. Looking through this scrapbook, I feel like I'm walking through the house of mirrors at a carnival. I get skinnier, fatter, shorter, taller . . . . I mean, I don't mind being named after Saint Nicholas—he was, after all, good and kind to children—but I don't look like him!"

He shows his elves an early picture of Saint Nicholas. "I ask you to look at that with objectivity. That gaunt, ascetic, sorrowful looking man—does that look like me?"

The elves know better than to answer. "And I may be good but I'm no saint, as all the bad little boys and girls will find out tomorrow night. Besides, artists pictured Saint Nicholas riding in a horse-drawn sleigh, and everybody knows about my reindeer.

"Then there's this chimney nonsense—all those artists who assumed that I had to be thin as a rail or as tiny as an elf (no offense, guys) to fit down the chimney. I don't know how they thought someone that small or frail could carry those sacks of toys and gifts. No, sir, I am a fellow of normal dimensions—well, maybe I've put some weight on over the years, but it is still the rare chimney that I can't squeeze through. If worse comes to worse, there are always my helpers, like the ever-svelte Knecht Ruprecht or Black Peter to slip down the narrowest flues.

"Nor am I the giant that the English suppose Father Christmas to be. They obviously confuse me with the ancient Ro-

man and Norse gods. Come winter's dark and cold, they want this huge figure to comfort and protect them. Well I've got news for them; I am merely man-sized, a healthy-sized man, but no giant. I am good for some trinkets and good cheer but they'll have to rely on providence and Mother Nature to rescue them from winter.

"Now about those fat jokes. I have quite a bone to pick with Doctor Moore and his 'Visit from St. Nicholas.' *'Twas the night before Christmas* indeed! Just look what he started way back in 1822 with those immortal lines:

> He had a broad face and a
>   little round belly
> That shook when he laughed
>   like a bowl full of jelly.
> He was chubby and plump,
>   a right jolly old elf . . .

I sound like I belong in a cookbook!

. . . and before you can say 'Haddon Sundblom's Coca-Cola Santa' all pictures of me showed this person who was as fat as a Christmas turkey. I mean, I don't have to take this kind of abuse. 'Queer looking hat' my aunt Martha!"

Santa is really heating up now, his jolly red glow firing to a crimson rush of indignation.

"Then, in the 1860's, Thomas Nast is picturing me rotund as one of his Republican elephants . . . and it snowballed from there! I think it was his drawings that inspired those lines in a children's book of the time . . .

> But Santa Claus comes in his
>   queer looking hat
> And we know he is good humoured
>   because he is fat.

"How would everyone feel if one Christmas I didn't show up at all? They would all get cards saying that Santa's sorry he couldn't come this year because he's at a fat farm! Don't these people realize it gets cold on those rooftops in December? A little bit of avoirdupois is essential. Let's face it. In the sleigh, what with the wind-chill factor and all, the red fur suit and the beard are just not enough.

"Perhaps the best idea would be, one year, to show up on the evening network news and say 'Enough speculation and rumor. This is me: this is what I really look like.' Reveal myself; end the misrepresentations and distortions once and for all." *Santa pauses a moment, ending his harangue. Then he shakes his head.*

"Naaaaaaaaah."

Michael Gross

⋅❧ Planning the Christmas Feast ❧⋅

Names of Family Members & Guests

Food to Be Served

☐ Turkey ☐ Roast beef ☐ Ham ☐ Other meat

☐ Stuffing for turkey: _____ and

for _____ casserole(s)

Recipe from: _____ page _____

Special ingredients: _____

_____

Served in what: _____

☐ Gravy: _____

Recipe from: _____ page _____

Special ingredients: _____

Served in what: _____

☐ Salad: _____

_____

Recipe from: _____ page _____

Special ingredients: _____

Served in what: _____

☐ Soup: _____

Recipe from: _____ page _____

Special ingredients: _____

_____

Served in what: _____

☐ Vegetables: _____

_____

_____

Recipe from: _____ page _____

Special ingredients: _____

Served in what: _____

☐ Sauces, Preserves & Pickles: _____

_____

Recipe from: _____ page _____

Recipe from: _____ page _____

Served in what: _____

☐ Desserts: _____

_____

Recipe from: _____ page _____

Recipe from: _____ page _____

Special ingredients: _____

Served in what: _____

☐ Beverages during meal: _____

_____

☐ Beverages after meal: _____

_____

What day it will be: _____ at

_____ o'clock, a.m./p.m.

Number of adults: _____ children: _____

How many tables needed: _____ chairs: _____

Who will sit where: _____

_____

Who is in charge of the kitchen: _____

Who are the kitchen helpers: _____

_____

Who will carve the meat: _____

Volunteers for dish-washing: _____

_____

Volunteers for cleaning up: _____

Who will set the table: _____

Who will do the table decorations: _____

_____

Shopping List to Copy Out

☐ Turkey: _____ lbs ☐ Roast beef: _____ lbs

☐ Ham: _____ lbs ☐ Other meat: _____ lbs

☐ Special ingredients

_____   _____

_____   _____

_____   _____

☐ Table decorations & candles

_____   _____

_____   _____

☐ Placecards

☐ Favors

_____   _____

_____   _____

☐ Utensils

_____   _____

_____   _____

☐ Serving Dishes

_____   _____

_____   _____

☐ Need to borrow: _____

_____

Preparation Checklist

☐ Order meat on _____

☐ Pick up meat on _____

☐ Shop for non-food items on _____

☐ Shop for food on _____

☐ Make _____

the week before

☐ Make _____

two days before

☐ Make _____

one day before

Criss-cross

The custom of using an X in the abbreviation *Xmas* for *Christmas* is neither secular nor irreligious. On the contrary, it goes back to early Christian times.

The name Christ means "the anointed" or "the messiah." In Greek, the sound *ch* or *kh* is represented by the letter X. Khristos was spelled X͞pictoc. Fifteen centuries ago X͞p was the common abbreviation for X͞pictoc; later Xt and simply X were used. A variant of the X was something like our plus sign, +.

Writers of children's alphabet books and horn books in the 16th and 17th centuries began the alphabet with a cross-like symbol meaning Christ, that only coincidentally suggested His death by crucifixion. This symbol looked like ✚. This led to a commonly used euphemism for the alphabet, "Christ-cross Row." As late as the mid-1860s, Charles Kingsley, author of *Water Babies,* described "twelve or fourteen neat, rosy, chubby little children, learning their Christ-cross row."

Any doubts about the propriety of the criss-cross abbreviation should be dispelled by so many centuries of approval for the form. Merry Xmas to you all!

Xmas Cross-Stitch Tablecloth

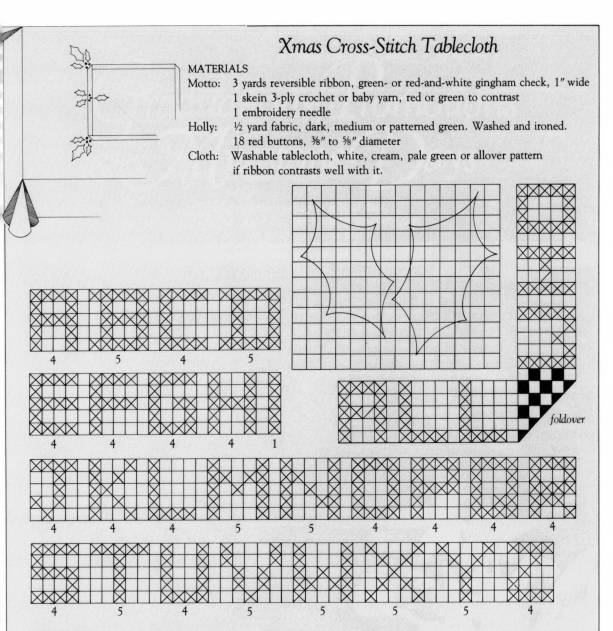

MATERIALS

Motto: 3 yards reversible ribbon, green- or red-and-white gingham check, 1″ wide
1 skein 3-ply crochet or baby yarn, red or green to contrast
1 embroidery needle

Holly: ½ yard fabric, dark, medium or patterned green. Washed and ironed.
18 red buttons, ⅜″ to ⅝″ diameter

Cloth: Washable tablecloth, white, cream, pale green or allover pattern if ribbon contrasts well with it.

DIRECTIONS

Each half of the motto uses about 40″ of 1″ ribbon. The ribbon here has 5 checks to the inch. Each letter (see alphabet above) is either 1, 4 or 5 units or checks wide by 5 high. Between each letter: 1 check; between each word: 2. On one length of ribbon (you may use the 4′ pieces sold in notions departments) cross stitch GOD BLESS ALL [10¾″] starting 3″ from end. Do the corner fold, then stitch WHO 'ROUND THIS CHRISTMAS [19¼″]. Corner fold, then TABLE DINE [9½″]. The other motto line starts 1″ from ribbon's end. Stitch MAY LOVE, HOPE [11″], corner fold, AND CHEER THROUGHOUT THE [21¾″], corner fold, YEAR BE THINE [11¼″]. Spacing cannot be equalized around the table, and there may be 2″ differences in the length of a side. Put tablecloth on table, center it, place motto ribbons with a yardstick as guide. Pin them down. Leave enough blank ribbon to fill gaps, turn ends under and stitch down. Cut out holly leaves; stitch the leaf veins with crochet yarn, and applique the leaves, turning edges under ¹/₁₆″. Sew on 3 buttons for berries with each group of 3 leaves. *Note: all measurements are approximate*

"... One word in conclusion. The best Christmas gift one can bestow on a child or friend is a happy memory. Money cannot buy it, but it may be procured by the poorest. It can be had by a draft upon patience or a check upon ill temper, which may be changed for the coin of kind words, each bearing the imprint, 'Peace on earth, good will to men.' "

From "The New York Times," December 23, 1894

Gifts

Our Stocking Stuffers

_____'s Stocking	_____'s Stocking
_____'s Stocking	_____'s Stocking
_____'s Stocking	_____'s Stocking

CHRISTMAS STOCKINGS
MENDED HEEL AND TOE

The stockings and socks in all
    different sizes
Are hung Christmas Eve to be filled
    with surprises:
For the nice there are nuts and some
    kind of fruit,
And perhaps a doll or a pull-toy
    to boot.
For the bad, a warning that good
    is the goal—
Down in the toe, a hard lump of coal.
There's pleasure for all in peanuts
    and pears
And anyone's large sock holds plenty
    of shares.
But even if someone little has been
    somewhat awful,
There's warmth for all too in a hard
    lump of coal.

Linda Campbell Franklin

Personalized Christmas Stockings

MATERIALS:

Red, green, bright blue, yellow, white and black *felt*—use 9" x 11¾" pieces from dimestore or larger pieces. Small bright *buttons*. Crochet or baby *yarn*. *Needlepoint needle*. Colored *threads* and *needle*, or white household *glue*. Brass *curtain rings*. *Ruler* and tailor's *chalk* or carbon *transfer paper*. *Pinking shears* or *scissors*.

DIRECTONS:

(1) For each stocking cut out two "socks" of felt. (2) Cut contrasting band, heel and toe. Top band might be scalloped or zig-zagged with pinking shears. Choose a design motif or (3) adapt a magazine picture by drawing a grid over it and redrawing on a smaller or larger grid drawn on paper. Cut out paper patterns and trace onto proper felt color. Cut out and turn over so chalk won't show. Sew or glue on design, bells, rick rack, eyes, etc., then assemble sock using (4) backstitch. Sew on curtain ring and hang. 9" x 11¾".

(1) sock shape   Each square = 1"

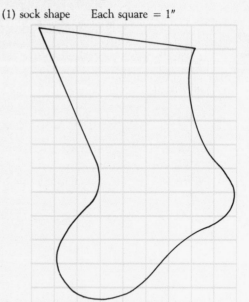

(4) backstitch

(2) various top bands, heels and toes

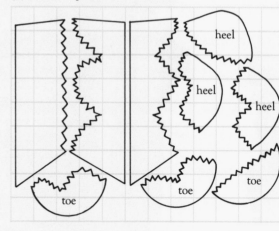

(3) gridded pictures

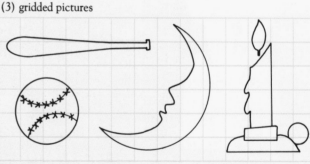

Twins

Polly:

There's such a lot that Santa Claus
    Must 'tend to when he b'gins.
I feel a little anxious, 'cause
    He might forget we're twins.

S'posen' he'd peek in at our bed
    "Bout 'leven or half-past-ten,
And say, "There's Dolly Brookses' head,
    And—Dolly Brooks again!"

And then he'd pull our stockings down.
    And shake his head, and say,
With such a dreadful stingy frown,
    "She can't fool me that way!"

Dolly:

Poor Polly wouldn't have a thing.
    How *terr'ble* that would be!
For every single toy he'd bring
    He'd s'pose would b'long to me.

Polly! let's take our picture-books
    Before we go to bed,
Marked "Polly Brooks" and "Dolly Brooks,"
    And hang them overhead.

Then, when old Santa comes our way,
    He'll smile the biggest grins,
And tiptoe 'round the bed, and say,
    "What have we here? Ah, twins!"

Caroline E. Condit, in "The Outlook," December 16, 1893

Boxing Day
'TWILL BE THE DAY AFTER CHRISTMAS

The British and Canadian custom of Boxing Day has nothing to do with the pugilistic arts. In fact, it is derived from a tradition of the English church. On December 26, which is the Feast of St. Stephen's, the church alms boxes are opened so that the money inside may be distributed among the poor. Over the years, there grew a tradition among servants and apprentices who took personal "Christmas boxes" around to their employers seeking tips and gratuities. These boxes were often rudely made of earthenware, and had a slit cut into the top to admit the coins. At the end of the day, the boxes were broken—like piggy banks. Presumably the person who received but a few pennies was encouraged to make an extra effort during the coming year.

A few days before Christmas, a letter was found in a *skrzynka pocztowa* in Gdańsk. Written on the envelope in big letters was the address: MR. SANTA CLAUS, North Poland. The *listonosz* who pulled the letter out of the *skrzynka pocztowa* had two *dzieci* at home, so he knew how important this letter was. He took out his pen and crossed off the address and he wrote *pilny!* in the corner. Then he wrote *Drogi Święty Mikołaju*, NORTH POLE. And he dropped it back in the *skrzynka pocztowa*. *Święty Mikołaju* got the letter just in time, and at the last minute, before he got in his sleigh, he took out one more *beben* and dropped it in his sack.

mailbox, postman, mailbox, children, urgent! Mr. Saint Nicholas, mailbox, Saint Nicholas, toy drum.

Dear Santa,

I WISH YOU
A JOLLY CHRISTMAS

Family Gift Chart

Fill in blanks, and let everyone in the family consult this before Christmas shopping.

Names								
Favorite colors								
Favorite hobby								
Favorite music								
Favorite perfume/aftershave								
Favorite doll/toy								
Favorite type of book								
Favorite flower								
Shirt/blouse size								
Pants/skirt size								
Dress size								
Underwear size								
Glove size								
Hat size								
Shoe size								
Ring size								
What my pet needs								
What I'd really like								

Gift Record

Gifts sent by us to faraway friends and relatives

Name	Gift

"The most essential thing for happiness is the gift of friendship."

Sir William Osler

Wishing you a merry Xmas

Decorate a Christmas Hat

Rings on the hatband?
Or bells on the brim?—
Here's a hat that's in need of
Some bright Christmas trim.

How about holly on the crown,
Or an ornament hung on the back?
What else do you imagine
This bonnet might lack?

Greenery
& Decoration

A Mexican Pesebre

The colorful figures at the left are part of a 20th century manger scene made of painted clay. It was made in Mexico, and like almost all crib or manger scenes, no matter where in the world they are made, it features standard figures: the Baby Jesus, a watchful Joseph and Mary, the angel with arm upraised as if to sing out an exultant "Hark!," the adoring Magi bearing their gifts of gold, frankincense and myrrh, and several of the stable animals. In addition, at the far right, are two figures, peasants—a man and woman, dressed in contemporary clothing, and holding gifts for the Child. It has been a tradition for at least four centuries for the creators of these scenes to include portrait figures of people from the area where the crib scene originates.

The various names for these scenes of the Birth of Christ include the French *crèche*, and manger or crib scene. All refer to the simple container used for fodder for the animals, freshly lined with straw to serve as a bed for the Baby Jesus.

Earl W. Kage, the New York state collector who has shared this handsome *pesebre* with us, has over 70 crib scenes. Every Christmas he lovingly unpacks this and others from all over the world and from many different ages. He follows a custom that exists everywhere of arranging the Three Wise Men at a distance, so that they may travel day by day towards Bethlehem, arriving on January 6.

On Christmas Eve, Mr. Kage invites a multitude of friends to take part in a beautiful tradition, during which 72 figures of the Baby Jesus are placed carefully and simultaneously in their cribs.

Making Your Own Manger Scene

ou do not need a ceramic kiln to make your own version of the Mexican *pesebre* on the preceding page. There are several products available at art supply stores at reasonable prices. One is called *Miracle Clay,* and can be baked in your kitchen oven between 150° and 300°F. Another brand which is fired in the kitchen oven is *Sculpey Modeling Compound.* A *self-setting modeling clay* that remains soft and workable until you are finished, and which air-dries to permanent hardness, comes in gray or terra-cotta. The last store-bought mixture is *Celluclay Papier Mache,* which is easily worked with hands or tools, and air-dries for permanency. If you use these products, follow the directions on the packages exactly. You can make the most basic figures in the crèche—the baby Jesus, the manger, Mary, Joseph, the Angel, the Three Kings, a shepherd, a camel, ox, burro and lamb—with about three pounds of modeling compound, provided you don't make the figures large.

An alternative to store-bought is a dough compound which can be baked in the oven. Homemade papier mâché can also be used, but it should be formed over paper and wire armatures—skeletons—because it takes so long to dry. The recipes for both are given here—it is up to you to experiment with the armatures.

DOUGH COMPOUND

4 cups flour, 1 cup salt, 2 tablespoons vegetable oil, 2 tablespoons hand lotion, about 2 cups water. Mix flour and salt; knead in oil, hand lotion and enough water to make a not-too-stiff dough. If you work slowly making the figures, store part of the mixture, covered, in the refrigerator. When figures are completed, bake for 60 minutes, at 225°F.

PAPIER MACHE PULP

Shred about 40 pages of newspaper into very small squares. Place them in a large pot until it is ¾ full. Add more paper shreds if there is room, lightly packing them in. Pour in enough water to make an easily-stirred mix. Cook over low heat, stirring occasionally. In about *six* hours, the paper will begin disintegrating. Cook another hour and let cool. Squeeze out excess water by pressing spoonsful in a large strainer. Spread the pulp on several layers of newspaper to drain overnight. Mix up a batch of wallpaper paste, or make your own "thick cream" flour-and-water paste, and add a few squirts of white household glue. Combine about three cups of pulp with one cup paste. Form human bodies over the tops of soda pop bottles, but remove to dry. Make crumpled paper, wire and masking tape skeletons for the animals.

No matter what material you use, the figures are all made approximately the same way. The directions here are for 3″ human figures, with the others in scale. the basic HUMAN BODY is made by rolling a 2″ long lump of clay into a slightly tapered cylinder. The head is a 1″ ball, rolled between the palms, and twist-stuck to the body. Arms, hair, robe sashes, etc., are made by rolling spaghetti lengths of clay or dough in varying thicknesses. Flat pieces, rolled flat with a rolling pin or straight-sided drinking glass, are made into shawls, crowns, stars, flowers, leaves and wings. Lips, noses, eyeballs, eyebrows and feet can be applied little bits of clay. Use a heavy needle, a #1 knitting needle, twigs, etc., to scratch fine details and hair.

The ANIMALS are made in a similar fashion. Bodies are rolled cylinders. Clay or plain papier mâché isn't strong enough for you to put a big fat body on long thin legs. Therefore, you will have to make fairly short tapering legs, and perhaps support the underside of the body with a paper cup, or a piece of waxed paper-covered clay, while the figure dries. Legs and tails are rolled. Eyes and details of mouths and nostrils are scratched, poked and applied.

Complete the figures and dry them according to package instructions. Paint with suitable paints—acrylics and latex work well.

It would be a lovely family tradition to add figures to the manger scene each year, including as many animals, trees and flowers as you wish, the inn keeper, the Fourth Wise Man from the short story, even, if you wish, the members of your own family.

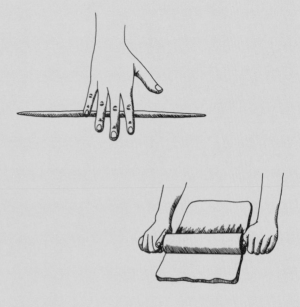

The Yule Log

The firey glow of a yule log is as comforting to Christians today as it must have been centuries ago to our pagan ancestors. It was a symbol of the sun, a prayer to the gods to light their way out of the darkness of winter, and bring back the green of spring. The yuletide season coincides with the celebration of the birth of Christ, and the yule log tradition, with its rich heritage of ritual was taken up by early Christians.

In the Northern countries, where the winters were long and very cold, the yule log was a strong symbol. In England, the rituals surrounding the bringing in of the yule log reached their height in medieval times. In some areas, the "Christmas Brand," as it was called, was dragged to the door by horses, and carried by as many people as it took to the fireplace, where it was bedded down for burning between Christmas Eve and the New Year, tended carefully and never allowed to go out. Often some sort of imprecation would be chanted while the log was lit with a piece of the last year's log. The following is one of the chants which we have record of:

Kindle the Christmas brand, and then
Til sunset let it burne;
Which quencht, then lay it up agen
Til Christmas next returne.

Part must be kept, wherewith to tend
The Christmas log next yeare;
And where tis safely kept, the fiend
Can do no mischief there.

In part of Germany, the *Christbrand* was a large block of wood, laid on the fire and burned only a short while—long enough to char. It was taken off and, when lightning on the fire as a protection for the house. threatened, the *Christbrand* was put back

Even in hot countries, like Italy and Greece, there is a long-standing tradition of burning a piece of wood at Christmas time. In Italy, wine was first poured over the log. In Greece, the much-feared, half-human, half-animal monsters called *Kallikantzaroi*, who wreak havoc in the house at Christmas time, are supposed to be kept away by the burning of the log.

Now we bring in a special log, saved from the woodpile, to burn on Christmas day. It gives such a cheery light, and seems to kindle extra warmth between members of the family and friends.

Superstitions
Surrounding the Yule Log

IT IS GOOD LUCK . . .

. . . to keep a piece of last year's log. It will protect your home from fire.

. . . to kindle this year's log from a piece of last year's.

. . . to obtain the log from your own property.

. . . to allow the log to burn continuously for the 12 days of Christmas.

. . . to use the ashes from the log as a cure for ailments, and a protection from hail.

. . . to mix the ashes in fodder, for it makes the cows calve.

. . . to drop some ashes in the well, for it makes the water sweet.

. . . to use the unburnt portion to make part of a plow, for it insures lush growth.

. . . for a guest to strike the burning log with a poker and say "For as many sparks come out of you, let there by as many oxen, horses, sheep, pigs and beehives?"

. . . for the log to light on the first try.

IT IS BAD LUCK . . .

. . . for a person with a squint to enter the room where the log is burning.

. . . for a barefoot person to enter.

. . . for a flatfooted woman to enter.

. . . to let the log burn all the way down.

. . . for the light from the fire to cast a headless shadow, for the person shall die within the year.

. . . to throw the ashes out on Christmas Day, for they might be thrown in the Christ Child's face.

. . . to buy the log.

. . . to give someone a branch kindled from the log and let them leave the house with it.

Our Wreath

Symbolizing eternal hope,
    the wreath goes 'round and 'round—
And where it starts or ends cannot be found.
Woven of things that grow—for life,
    and hung for holiday delight.
The wreath must be left in place
    from Christmas Eve through Twelfth Night

Who made it _____

What is it made of? _____

_____

Our Tree

Who decorated it _____

_____

The oldest ornament is _____

_____

Christmas Greetings

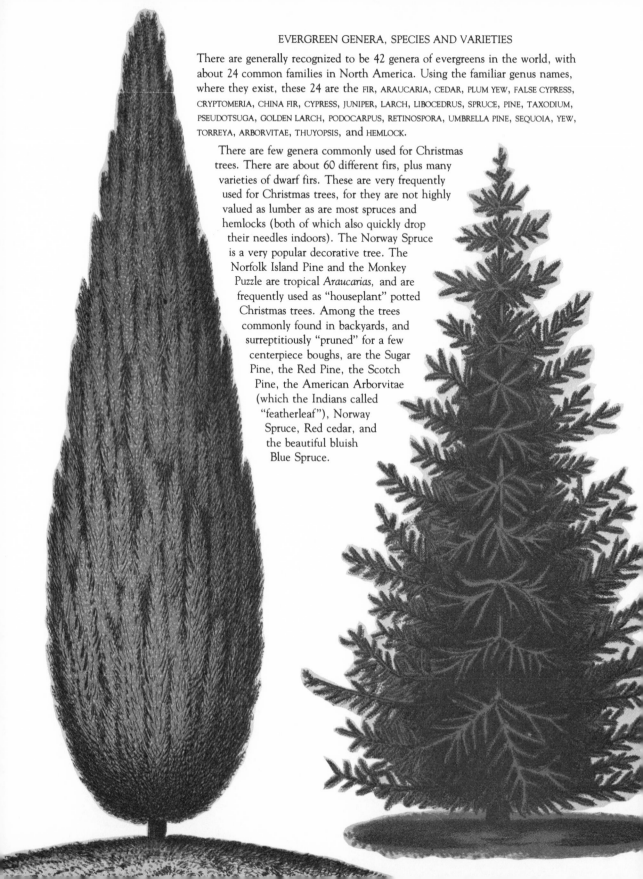

EVERGREEN GENERA, SPECIES AND VARIETIES

There are generally recognized to be 42 genera of evergreens in the world, with about 24 common families in North America. Using the familiar genus names, where they exist, these 24 are the FIR, ARAUCARIA, CEDAR, PLUM YEW, FALSE CYPRESS, CRYPTOMERIA, CHINA FIR, CYPRESS, JUNIPER, LARCH, LIBOCEDRUS, SPRUCE, PINE, TAXODIUM, PSEUDOTSUGA, GOLDEN LARCH, PODOCARPUS, RETINOSPORA, UMBRELLA PINE, SEQUOIA, YEW, TORREYA, ARBORVITAE, THUYOPSIS, and HEMLOCK.

There are few genera commonly used for Christmas trees. There are about 60 different firs, plus many varieties of dwarf firs. These are very frequently used for Christmas trees, for they are not highly valued as lumber as are most spruces and hemlocks (both of which also quickly drop their needles indoors). The Norway Spruce is a very popular decorative tree. The Norfolk Island Pine and the Monkey Puzzle are tropical *Araucarias*, and are frequently used as "houseplant" potted Christmas trees. Among the trees commonly found in backyards, and surreptitiously "pruned" for a few centerpiece boughs, are the Sugar Pine, the Red Pine, the Scotch Pine, the American Arborvitae (which the Indians called "featherleaf"), Norway Spruce, Red cedar, and the beautiful bluish Blue Spruce.

Evergreens

The archetypical Christmas tree is an evergreen that is conical in shape as well as generously coniferous—or cone-bearing. The pine, the fir and the spruce are the most well-known Christmas evergreens in North America. According to one ancient legend, the first Christmas tree was a living fir. Saint Winifred, who lived in the eighth century, tried to persuade the heathens around him to worship one God rather than a multitude of gods. One day, as the story goes, he chopped down their great oak tree, the symbol of their thunder god, and in its place there immediately appeared a tall, strong fir. Saint Winifred pointed to the tree and told the amazed crowd that this was the symbol of the living God.

The pine tree, according to even more ancient legend, was first a flirtatious shepherd who was turned into a pine by Cybele, the mother of the gods, because of her jealousy. Cybele had deeply loved the shepherd, and she mourned him night after day by lying beneath the branches of the pine. The god Jove felt such sympathy for her that he caused the foliage of the pine to remain forever green.

Because for thousands of years evergreen trees were worshipped and surrounded by legend to explain their lasting greenness, it was natural for early Christians to identify the tree that never died with the living Christ. During the early Middle Ages, celebrations of the birth of Jesus were accompanied by decorations of boughs of various symbolic plants, holly, mistletoe and evergreen among them. However, it was probably not until around 1600 that the practice began of bringing into the house a whole tree, and decorating it for Christmas. According to Clement Miles, in *Christmas Customs and Traditions*, ". . . the first historical mention of the Christmas-tree is found in the notes of a certain Strasburg [Germany] citizen of unknown name, written in . . . 1605. 'At Christmas they set up fir-trees in the parlours . . . and hang thereon roses cut out of many-coloured paper, apples, wafers, gold-foil, sweets, &c.' "

Nowadays, we are all familiar with the sight of Christmas tree farms, and springy rows of cord-bound trees of all sizes laid against buildings and panel trucks for sale to people who have no place to chop down (or dig up) their own Christmas trees. The growing practice—and a wonderful one it is, in keeping with the spirit of this special holiday— is to buy a living tree to bring into your home for a week or so, before being taken outside for planting. If kept watered, and protected from heat, and if planted carefully according to the instructions of the nurseryman, these living trees are growing proof of the joys of Christmases past.

Animal-Shaped Christmas Tree Ornaments

The household pets shown at the right, including a surprisingly calm cat, are late Victorian, embossed cardboard, fully three-dimensional Christmas tree ornaments. They were made between 1880 and 1910 in Dresden, Germany. They are only four animals from a fabulous collection of all kinds of ornaments and other Christmas artifacts belonging to Phillip Snyder of New York. Not only did the Dresden artisans make realistically painted figures of dogs and cats, they created many other pressed cardboard animals, including a variety of fish, horses, camels, polar bears, elephants, geese, storks, ducks, owls and peacocks—most of which were not painted but finished with a layer of gold or silver paper.

There are many other antique and newer ornaments in the shape of animals. This is not surprising because of the association of barnyard animals with the manger in Bethlehem, and because of the early practice of decorating trees with small toy animals. Some of the forms to look for are delicate blown glass cats and dogs, pigs, elephants, fish and birds, made by the glass-blowers of Lauscha, Germany. Simple ball ornaments were being made there by the 1840s, but not for a number of years were ornaments blown in the shape of animals. Well-known are the birds with spun-glass tails, fastened to tree branches by means of a spring clip.

Not too long after the coming of electricity, small blown-molded bulbs in many shapes were made for decorating trees. First blown in Austria at the turn of the century, the animals, birds, fruits and flowers were soon being copied in America and Japan, by hand and then by machine. The Japanese made clear and "milk" glass bulbs, in forms such as a cat playing a fiddle, a monkey with a large ball, birds in cages, parrots, very tubby cats, even Little Orphan Annie's Sandy.

In the late 1920s, a short-lived industry manufacturing figural bulbs from molded celluloid started up. Swans, storks, roosters, fish, bears, cats and dogs were all finely detailed, but also highly flammable. They often burst into flames as soon as the bulb heated up.

Among the most recent figural glass bulbs sought by collectors are a boxed set of seven unauthorized Disney characters from around 1960. They are humorous but poor representations of some of Walt Disney's most famous animals: Mickey and Minnie, Pluto, Donald Duck and Jiminy Cricket.

For further reading: The Christmas Tree Book *by Phillip V. Snyder, 1976.*

The Animal Kingdom

THE BUNWINKIES CHRISTMAS TREE

— Inez Tribit.

In a hollow at one end of the Wide-Wild-Wood lived Rab Rabbit Bunwinkie, his wife, Abbie Bunwinkie, and three young Bunwinkies, Bobbit, Babbit and little Babette. In the gray farmhouse at the other end of the Wide-Wild-Wood lived Father and Mother Goodlove and three young Goodloves, Chippy, Chappy and little Cuddlekin.

Now the young Bunwinkies like to watch the Goodlove children and listen to their chatter and then try to carry out in their own lives some of the things that they had learned.

One day in white December weather, Bobbit and Babbit Bunwinkie came skipping home with a big piece of news.

"Christmas is coming!" shouted Bobbitt with his eyes as big as his news.

"Christmas is coming!" echoed Babbit, with never a moment to lose.

"What's Christmas!" asked little Babette.

"Why, Christmas is when you hang up your stockings," danced Bobbit.

"And get presents in them," pranced Babbit.

"But, my darlings," put in Mother Bunwinkie, "your stockings won't come off, so how can you hang them anywhere?"

"That would be a poor habit," murmured Father Rab Rabbit.

Bobbit and Babbit glanced at their brown furry paws. "Then we can't have any presents at all, I suppose," doubted Bobbit.

"No, we can't have any presents at all," pouted Babbit.

"But what are presents?" puzzled little Babette.

"Why, new things to wear," answered Bobbit spryly.

"And new things to eat," added Babbit shyly.

"But, my dears," laughed Mother Bunwinkie, "what do you want of new things to wear? Your clothes never give out and you keep one suit forever. And what do you need to eat? Why stuff more eatables into stockings, I say, when our cupboard is overflowing with goodies already?"

"But the Goodloves have new playthings, too," clamored Bobbit."
"Yes, the—the—children—have—have—new—playthings, too," stammered Babbit.
"What are playthings?" wondered Babette.
"Why, spinning-tops and jumping-jacks," chimed Bobbit lightly.
"And skipping-ropes and trains on tracks," rhymed Babbit brightly.
"Oh, my! Oh, my, my lambkins!" smiled Mother Bunwinkie, "why do you pine for playthings? Haven't you four legs apiece on which to spin and jump and skip? Playthings indeed! Tut, Tut! You have yours always with you, and don't have to take them out, or put them away."
"And if we have no stockings to hang, we sha'n't have to have anything to tuck into them: that's a comfort, isn't it?" spoke up Father Rab Rabbit cheerfully.
"Well, perhaps so," returned Bobbit and Babbit tearfully.
But the very next day in they hopped with some brand-new news.
"The Goodloves are going to have a Christmas tree," sang Bobbit.
"What's a Christmas tree?" questioned Babette.
"An evergreen tree that you cut down and take into your house," explained Bobbit.
"And dress up with shiny stuff that looks like snow and ice," exclaimed Babbit. "Then on Christmas Eve you have a party around your tree."
"What a singular habit," frowned Father Rab Rabbit.
"Now, now, my rabbits," chaffed Mother Bunwinkie, "our little home isn't big enough to hold a tree, and what's the use of wasting a fine little evergreen by chopping it down and hauling it into a place where it will droop and die when it has so much more space and air and sunshine and will last so much longer out-of-doors? Tut, tut! A tree in a house, indeed!"
"A mischievous habit," mourned father Rab Rabbit.
"But why can't we have an out-doors tree, then?" piped up little Babette.
"The very thing!" approved Mother Bunwinkie.
"Oh, yes! Oh, yes! Let's choose that little fir at the edge of the Wood," called Bobbit and Babbit like one little rabbit.
"But what shall we do for trimmings?" cried Bobbit.
"What shall we do for shiny stuff like snow and ice?" sighed Babbit.
"Wait and see," smiled Mother Bunwinkie wisely.
And that very night came a snow storm and a blow storm. The white flakes flew and the wild winds blew, and in the morning there stood the little fir tree robed in soft, fluffy down, from its foot to its crown. Besides, that afternoon the clouds scattered a host of sleety raindrops over the earth, and before long the tips of the branches of the little fir were hung with tiny, tinkling icicles. So when the sun shone out the next day it set the snow and ice all a-glitter and a-dazzle with diamonds.
"Oh, good enough!" beamed Bobbit.
"Here's our shiny stuff," gleamed Babbit.
"Who'd long for shams when we can have the real thing?" gloated Mother Bunwinkie.
"Not we! Not we!" declared Bunwinkies three.
"But where are the candles!" queried little Babette.

"Wait and see," quoth Mother Bunwinkie again.

And that very night, into the clear sky came the moon and the stars, and they shed their radiance over the fir tree until it glimmered and shimmered and glistened almost as gorgeously as it had in the sunshine.

"Who'd wish for wax tapers and electric bulbs when he can have all the lights of heaven for his tree?" rejoiced Mother Bunwinkie.

"Not we!' Not we!" crowed Bunwinkies three.

"But now where is our party?" inquired Babette.

"Wait and see," advised Mother Bunwinkie again.

And on Christmas Eve there came flocking to the Bunwinkies' Christmas tree many of the folk of the Wide-Wild-Wood. There was the wonderful Wise White Owl, with Miles Mink, Reck Raccoon, Willy Woodchuck, Quirlie Gray Squirrel, and two or three winter birds—and there was the party!

The merry company danced round the tree and played "Blind-Bunny-Buff," "Hare in the Hollow," "Chase the Squirrel," and other jolly games. For refreshments there were rose-hips, wintergreen-leaves, dried apples, and other dainties from Mother Bunwinkie's well-stocked cupboard.

When the moon went down and the guests went home, Father Rab Rabbit said, "Let's run over and have a peep at the Goodlove's Christmas tree."

So away stole the Bunwinkie family through the wood to an unshaded window in the living-room of the old gray farmhouse. They scraped the frost from the pane and then they could see the little tree that had been borne away from the Wide-Wild-Wood. It was sad and drooping now.

Its lights were burned out, and it was stripped of its treasures. The floor was strewn with scattered games, broken toys and torn scraps of paper.

"How much wiser rabbits are than human beings," whispered Mother Bunwinkie. "Our tree cost us nothing and made us no trouble at all, and now we have no putting in order to do and nothing to give us a care. People think they must have lots of things to make them happy, but we rabbits enjoy ourselves with what we find about us."

"A sensible habit," nodded Father Rab Rabbit. Then the Bunwinkies all scampered home to bed.

Martha Burr Banks, from Little Folks: The Childrens Magazine, *December 1916*

Suet for the Birds

Because of their rapid heart beat and the need for constant fuel in order to keep warm, wintering birds should be supplied with extra food during the cold weather. Once started, this help should be regular— sometimes several times a day— because the birds come to depend on you.

The recipe here is simple. After experimentation, you will discover what the stayover birds in your area want in their suet cakes. Because suet primarily appeals to insect-eating species, do not take away your plain seed mixtures, even though seeds are mixed in with the suet. When it's "for the birds," many supermarkets will give you large chunks of suet free of charge; others package it and charge. If possible, have your butcher grind the suet into small pieces to make it melt easier.

In a skillet, melt the suet and stir in a variety of seeds including hemp, millet, sunflower and others in a wild bird seed mixture. You may also add raisins, corn meal, chopped unsalted peanuts, even cooked spaghetti. You have at least 20 minutes before the suet congeals.

There are several ways to serve the mixture. Pour it to fill the spaces around the petals of a large open pine cone, or dip smaller pine cones in the mixture. Bore shallow holes in a length of tree branch and fill them with suet. Fill half a coconut shell, or stir the mixture with an evergreen bough to coat the needles. A good hanging server is made from half-inch mesh wire netting. Cut a 10″ x 12″ piece, taking care that no sharp, hard-to-see wires are sticking out. Bend the netting over to make a 4″ x 10″ cylinder and squash it so there are only a couple of inches space inside. Lay the cylinder in an oblong cake pan and pour the suet over it. Let it congeal. Hang the suet cage from a low branch, or tack it to the north side of a tree trunk, five or six feet from the ground to encourage groundfeeders and discourage dogs. Grateful wintering birds include chickadees, nuthatches, woodpeckers, juncos, cardinals, towhees, wrens, blue jays and sparrows.

CHIRPING PARTY MENU: Unsalted peanut butter spread thinly on bark, cracked corn, frozen pokeberries (poisonous to humans, so label for your freezer carefully), oranges, bananas, apple peelings, bread crumbs, and sand, grit or finely crushed oyster shells.

The custom in Hungary, Germany and Sweden for many centuries was to save the last sheaf of wheat from the harvest in the fall, and feed it to the wild birds during Christmas week.

A Santa Claus Play

SANTA: *Now children, I am going to own up—I was right
down-spirited, but you are putting me in tiptop
frame of mind again. This makes me think: I will
tell you a little incident that happened the other
day. I said to Mrs. Santa, says I:*

One day out of spirits, I said to my wife,
"I'm tired of the reindeer, I am on my life;
For you know that we live in an up-to-date age
And that motors and airships are now all the rage;
And I take such long rides I'm beginning to feel
That I really should get me an automobile."
But dear Mrs. Santa in doubt shook her head;
"You better stick to the reindeer," she said;
"You can't drive an auto, you'll sure have a wreck,
And the next thing I know you'll be breaking your neck;
So Santa just take the advice of your wife,
And stick to the reindeer the rest of your life."

But Santa is stubborn, you know some men are;
And the day before Christmas I bought me a car,
And I piled in the bags and the bundles of toys
That my wife had helped make for the girls and the boys.
And I wondered a little at how they would feel
When they knew I was sporting an automobile.
Then I cranked up my car, to my wife said good-day,
And with tooting of horn I was off and away.
But my good wife sighed and said, "Whew, how it smells!
I wish you would stick to the reindeer and bells."

Now Santa tore off through the ice and the snow,
And you may be sure I did not go slow;
My teeth fairly chattered and blue was my nose,
And the icicles soon on my long whiskers froze.
And I said to myself as I shivered the while,
"It's rather uncomfortable putting on style."
But I soon had to learn that an automobile
Sometimes springs a surprise on the man at the wheel;
For I punctured a tire on a sharp bit of ice,
And the car and the toys were upset in a trice;
And what happened then? Of course you all know,
I was planted head first in a deep drift of snow.

While I scrambled and sputtered and dug myself out,
My car was a wreck, the toys scattered about,
And I said to myself, "Well, I have been a dunce."
Then I called up my wife on the wireless at once;
"Hurry up and drive down with the reindeer and sled,
I've had a mishap," was all that I said.

With a clatter of hooves and a shiver of cold
Mrs. Santa arrived and my story I told,
And while in the sleigh we were packing the toys,
She said: "I am glad that the girls and the boys
Who watch and who wait for your coming this year
Will know you're still driving the little reindeer,
For I know just how sorry the children would feel
To have them turned down for an automobile,
And as for the auto, why bless your old heart,
Right after Christmas we'll take it apart,
And when we've disposed of the smell and the noise
We will work it up into a fine lot of toys.
But you must away—take this message with you:
Tell the children to always be loving and true,
Give each one a candle to help make things bright,
And tell them to try and live up to the light."

CHILDREN: *Santa Claus running an automobile?*
Only just think how we children would feel!
Why, just before Christmas we all love to hear
How Santa Claus comes with his little reindeer,
And we can't give them up for an auto, you know.
On, no, no, no! We can't have it so!

SANTA: *"Well, well, bless my soul! who ever thought*
that the boys and girls were so fond of the
reindeer—"

CHILDREN: *"Well we are, we are—"*

SANTA: *"And you don't want old Santa to be up to*
date and have an automobile like all the rest of
the world?"

CHILDREN: *"No, no, no, we can't have it so!"*

SANTA: *"But you must remember that reindeer have to*
be fed and watered and taken care of, and
that's quite a task—"

CHILDREN: *"Yes, of course, we know, but—"*

SANTA: *"And it won't do to forget them and let them*
go cold and hungry—"

CHILDREN: *"No, of course that won't do."*

SANTA: *"Well, then, if you never forget to feed and*
care for your pet animals—guess I can afford to
take care of the reindeer."

CHILDREN: *"We will promise to take care of our pets; we*
will, we will!"

SANTA: *"Well, bless you, that's good! That's a good*
Christmas bargain. Now, you boys and girls
want to remember that 'Love and kindness to
every living creature' is the watchword from
now on."

CHILDREN: *"Dear Santa, we will bear in mind,*
To all things living to be kind;
To all our pets, to birds that sing,
And every little furry thing,

And love and kindness, Santa dear,
Shall be our watchword, all the year;
To do some little kindly deed,
To help someone in time of need,
No opportunity we'll miss;
We promise this—we promise this."

Elizabeth Clarke Hardy in "Santa Claus and the
Christmas Candles," 1911

Celebration & Traditions

Merry Christmas

The Twelve or Thirteen Days of Christmas

The Christmas season begins at different times in different countries. According to the Roman Catholic Church, the season begins with Advent Sunday, four Sundays before Christmas Eve. St. Nicholas' Day on December 6 is often used as a starting date for the celebration of the season. In Sweden, St. Lucia's Day on the 13th of December signals the beginning. However, there *is* common to most of Christendom, a period known either as the Twelve or Thirteen Days of Christmas.

This period begins on Christmas Eve and ends on Epiphany, the day often celebrated as the anniversary of the arrival of the three wise men, the Magi, at the stable in Bethlehem, bearing gifts for the child Jesus. In fact, the holiday is sometimes called Three Kings Day.

In England, the counting does not include Christmas Day itself, and so Epiphany, which falls on January 6, is called "Twelfth Day." In Germany, Holland, Belgium and parts of Sweden, Christmas Day *is* counted, and Epiphany is therefore "Thirteenth Day." In those countries, Twelfth Night falls on the eve of Epiphany, that is, on January 5. This accounts for the confusion in America concerning Twelfth Night and Twelfth Day. People here come from all over the world, each bringing their different heritage of Christmas. In fact, in some countries, January 6 is supposed to be the anniversary of the baptism of Jesus, while the Vatican celebrates baptism day on January 9.

At any rate, the days and nights of Christmastide are mingled celebrations of the birth of Jesus, the arrival of the New Year, a feast time, a turning from the dead of winter to the expectation of new life in spring, and a time for prayer and thanksgiving as well as merriment and good cheer.

Winter Sports
FOR SAFETY'S SAKE

Don't go skating, skiing, sledding or snowshoeing alone. Tell someone where you are going, and when you plan to return.

Plan beforehand what to do if you get separated from your companions, or if all of you get lost.

Split up the food and hot drinks so that everyone is carrying a supply which, in case of an accident, could help keep him warm.

Dress in layers. Several layers, even of cotton, starting with cotton or wool thermal underwear, are warmer than one layer of wool or fur. Manmade knits are not preferred.

Return home, even if your companions beg you to stay, if you get wet or injure yourself. The chills of hypothermia, when the body's temperature drops dangerously low, are extremely dangerous and can come on quickly and without warning.

Do not ski or sled on slopes too advanced for your skill. Likewise, do not show off on any slope—it endangers yourself and others.

Do not skate on ponds, streams, rivers or lakes unless the ice is thick enough. Two inches is usually thick enough, but three or more inches are better. The police department in most communities can tell you when it's safe. Carrying a hockey stick can actually be very helpful, even if you are not playing ice hockey. It can be used to pull another skater out of a hole. If grasped with both hands in a horizontal position, if you feel yourself falling through the ice, it may serve as a brace on either side of the hole and keep you up until someone can crawl close enough to extend a stick or long scarf or something else to drag you out.

In areas where there is heavy, overhanging snow and steep slopes, do not for fun try to start an avalanche by shouting. Leave the area instead.

Don't ignore danger signals from your body or your friends'. Unstoppable shivering, teeth chattering, blue lips, blue or white-tipped fingers, noses and toes, snow blindness, etc., are all things which mean you should get indoors. Seek shelter if you cannot go home. Put on a Mylar space blanket—they radiate the heat being lost by the body, back where it's needed. Do not try to warm up fingers or faces by covering them with snow. Remember that snow is frozen! On the other hand, should all other shelter be lacking, and someone needs protection from wind while you go for help, a windscreen can be quickly built from snow.

Do not drink alcoholic beverages. The sense of warmth and well-being is illusory. Hot chocolate, hot sweet coffee or coffee-like cereal beverages are much more helpful. See the recipe on page 16.

Do not pack hard, icy snowballs from wet snow and throw them at friends in a snowball fight. They are lethal. They can cause unconsciousness, knock out teeth, break noses, and do other un-fun things.

Make sure your equipment fits you. Boots and shoes should be snug enough to give support (particularly for skiing or skating), but not so tight as to cut off circulation. Skis should be the right length for downhill or cross-country. Bindings should be the kind which break away if you fall. Don't use antique "beartrap" ski bindings to complete an old-fashioned sporting look.

The Night Before Christmas; A Visit from St. Nicholas

'Twas the [night] [be]4 Christmas, w[hen] [house]
[knot] a creature was stirr[ing], [not] even a [mouse];
The [stockings] were hung by the chim[ney] with care,
In hopes t[hat] St. Nicholas soon [would be] there;

The children were [nest][sled] [pepper] snug in their [beds],
While visions of sugar-plums danced in their heads;
[And] Mamma in her kerchief, [and] [I] in my cap,
Had just settled our brains 4 a long winter's nap,

W[hen] out on the lawn there [rose] such a c[latter],
[I] sprang from the [bed] 2 see w[hat] was the matter.
Away 2 the window [I] flew like a flash,
Tore open the shutters [and] threw [up] the sash.

The [moon] on the breast of the [new]-fallen snow
Gave the lustre of midday 2 objects [be]low,
W[hen], w[hat] 2 my [wondering] ii should [appear],
But a miniature sleigh, [and] 8 [tiny] reindeer,

With a little old driver, so lively [and] quick,
[I] [knew] in a moment it must [be] St. Nick.
More rapid than [eagles] [eagles] his [coursers] they came,
[And] he whistled, [and] shouted, [and] called them by name:

"Now, *Dasher*! now, *Dancer*! now, *Prancer* [and] *Vixen*!
On *Comet*! on, *Cupid*! on, *Donner* [and] *Blitzen*!
2 the [top] of the porch! 2 the [top] of the wall!
Now dash away! dash away! dash away [all]!"

As dry leaves t[hat] [be]4 the wild hurri[cane] [fly],
W[hen] they meet with an obstacle, mount 2 the sky,
So [up] 2 the house-[top] the [coursers] they flew,
With the sleigh full of [toys] [and] St. Nicholas 2.

✳ t🐦, in a twinkl🔔, 👁 heard on the roof
The pranc🔔 ✳ paw🔔 of each little hoof.
As 👁 drew in my head, ✳ was turn🔔 around,
↓ the chim/🦅 St. Nicholas came with a bound.

He was 👗ed 🗡 in fur, from his head **2** his foot,
✳ his clothes were 🗡 tarnished with ashes ✳ soot;
A bundle of 🧸 he had flung on his back,
✳ he looked like a pedlar just o/🔔 his pack.

His **i i**—how they twinkled! his dimples how merry!
His cheeks were like 🌹🌹, his nose like a cherry!
His droll little mouth was drawn ↑ like a 🎀,
✳ the beard of his chin was as white as the snow;

The 🪺 of a 🥖 he held tight in his 🦷,
✳ the smoke it encircled his head like a wreath;
He had a broad face ✳ a little round 🔔y,
T🎩 s🪝 w🐦 he laughed, like a bowlful of jelly.

He was chubby ✳ plump, a right jolly old elf,
✳ 👁 laughed w🐦 👁 🗝 him, in spite of myself;
A wink of his **i** ✳ a twist of his head
Soon gave me **2** know 👁 had nothing to dread.

He spoke 🪢 a word, but went straight **2** his work,
✳ filled 🗡 the 🧦; t🐦 turned with a jerk,
✳ laying his finger aside of his nose,
✳ giving a nod, ↑ the chim/🦅 he 🌹;

He sprang **2** his sleigh, **2** his team gave a whistle,
✳ away they 🗡 flew like the ↓ of a 🌿.
But 👁 heard him exclaim, ere he drove out of sight,

HAPPY CHRISTMAS TO ALL
AND TO ALL A GOOD NIGHT!

Clement Moore, 1822   *Rebus version by L. C. Franklin*

Our Christmas Eve

Who Shared Christmas Eve Together

What We Did

Menu

Our Traditions on Christmas Eve

Special Christmas Eve Presents

What We Left for Santa Claus

Our Christmas Day

Who Was Together on Christmas Day

How We Spent Christmas Before the Feast

A _____ Family Christmas Story

First of all, _____ got up earliest at _____ o'clock, and _____ was late

getting out of _____ and pretended not to hear the _____ . Everyone was in the _____ ,

sitting around wearing _____ , wishing that _____ would get started! Only

one _____ burned, so it was given to _____ . At _____ o'clock, the first

_____ was opened. It was for _____ , from _____ .

_____ smiled and said " _____ !" We began basting the

turkey every _____ minutes, so that it would be ready to eat at _____ o'clock. We thought of several things

which could go wrong: _____ , _____ and _____ . But–

surprise! surprise!–_____ happened. Outside we could see that it was _____ ,

even though the weatherman said it would _____ . Christmas night we all _____ ,

and said to each other what a _____ , _____ , _____ ,

_____ , _____ day it had been. _____ to all, and to all

a _____ !

Breakfast Menu

Late Night Snacks

Birds at the Feeder on Christmas

What We Did after Dinner

Special Family Christmas Day Traditions

Joyful Christmas

BEST CHRISTMAS WISHES

Visitors at Christmas Time

By
Telephone

In touch—by calling on the 'phone,
Or dropping by our happy home—
Our friends and family from far and near
Share the lovely warmth of Christmas cheer!

In Person

A Prayer at Christmas

ear Lord, At this time of celebration of the birth long ago of Jesus the Nazarene, who symbolizes for millions the embodiment of love, kindness, and other virtues that humans can recognize and try to attain, let us pray to the spirit of goodness that exists in every creature. Let us try to understand and nourish a love for all who share this beautiful planet that spins so smoothly through limitless space.

Let us remind ourselves throughout the year, on this and other birthdays, that all our acts and habits of thought have consequences upon ourselves and often upon others, bringing joy or misery. Knowing that none of us is perfect, that everyone is a mixture, let us try to recognize what is good, and work for what we believe will be fair and helpful to all, not forgetting the creatures like whales and butterflies and puppies and trees, whose lives and growth and generation will often depend on what we humans decide or do.

Let us realize that each of us in our own way is responsible for all great accomplishments and the terrible mistakes of human society. Let us realize that just as the immense harvests that feed the world begin with individual tiny seeds, so each of us shares the responsibility and will meet the consequences of the acts of our governments, corporations, churches and all other associations.

Let us take joy together in the lovely miracles of life, and as we celebrate, resolve inwardly to come closer to the ideals set by those great souls, famed or humble, whoever they may be, that you and I inwardly revere. *Amen.* *Robert D. Franklin*

The News at Christmas Time

_____ , 198 ___

'Tis the morning of Christmas,
And all through the news,
Are pictures and stories
Full of Christmas Eve clues.
And the day after Christmas
Give the paper another look
For headlines and articles
To paste in this book!

Christmas Eve News

The name of our paper _____

Christmas Day News

The name of our paper _____

Tad Lincoln's Turkey

The following story concerns Tad Lincoln, the President's son, who died in 1871 at the age of 18. The story was recounted for the editor of The Everyday Life of Abraham Lincoln, *Francis F. Browne, for publication in 1896.*

A friend of the Lincoln family once sent a fine live turkey to the White House, with the request that it should be served on the President's Christmas table. But Christmas was then several weeks off, and in the interim Tad won the confidence and esteem of the turkey, as he did the affection of every living thing with which he came in contact. 'Jack,' as the fowl had been named, was an object of great interest to Tad, who fed him, petted him, and began to teach him to follow his young master. One day, just before Christmas, 1863, while the President was engaged with one of his Cabinet ministers on an affair of great moment, Tad burst into the room like a bombshell, sobbing and crying with rage and indignation. The turkey was about to be killed. Tad had procured from the executioner a stay of proceedings while he flew to lay the case before the President. Jack must not be killed; it was wicked. 'But,' said the President, 'Jack was sent here to be killed and eaten for this very Christmas.' 'I can't help it,' roared Tad, between his sobs. 'He's a good turkey, and I don't want him killed.' The President of the United States, pausing in the midst of his business, took a card and wrote on it an order of reprieve. The turkey's life was spared, and Tad, seizing the precious bit of paper, fled to set him at liberty."

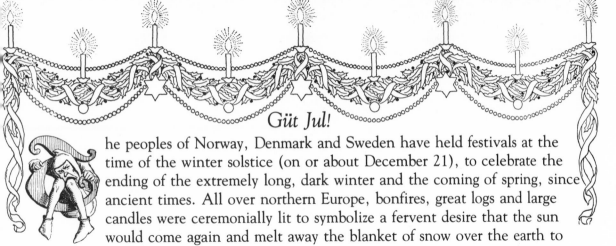

Güt Jul!

he peoples of Norway, Denmark and Sweden have held festivals at the time of the winter solstice (on or about December 21), to celebrate the ending of the extremely long, dark winter and the coming of spring, since ancient times. All over northern Europe, bonfires, great logs and large candles were ceremonially lit to symbolize a fervent desire that the sun would come again and melt away the blanket of snow over the earth to allow the planting of crops.

These Northern traditions have been thoroughly integrated into the Scandanavian celebration of Christmas, but like the word *jul* (which may either mean a month near the winter solstice, or a wheel—signifying the revolving seasons), they predate Christmas. The *jul* is as old as northern European man's consciousness of a cyclical "calendar."

All over Scandinavia, food is left out in the snow as offerings to *Jul* beings, just as seeds and sheaves of wheat are left for the birds. In Denmark, where the traditional Christmas Eve meal begins with rice pudding, some of the pudding is left outside for the *Julnissen*—to insure the good will of the elves who inhabit the haylofts and guard people's homes.

Swedes have their own hayloft elf, the *Jultomten*. He was borrowed in the last century or so from mythology, and is supposed to deliver Christmas gifts, in a sleigh drawn by a *Julbock*, a goat which belonged to Thor! *Jultomtens* are related to Norway's *Julsvenn*, who long ago delivered lucky barley stalks to insure a good harvest, but who now represents a Santa-like personage who brings Christmas gifts.

As an important holiday of the *Jul* season, probably nothing ranks higher in Scandinavia than the Festival of St. Lucia, on December 13. This is a Swedish feast day, although St. Lucia herself was a Sicilian martyr of the fourth century. Her day is known as "little yule," and marks the beginning of the Christmas season in Sweden. It starts around four or five a.m. with a daughter of the house donning a white dress and a crown of nine lit candles, fastened to whortleberry twigs. She visits the members of the sleeping household, each in their own room, and awakens them with coffee, buns and cake.

The coincidence of the winter solstice and the birth of Christ is a happy one—and probably nowhere in the world could Christians make so much use of older pagan traditions to celebrate the new religion than in Scandinavia. It is difficult for many of us to imagine Christmas time as anything but a snowy cold time—songs like "I'm Dreaming of a White Christmas" and the carol about Good King Wenceslaus, looking out over snow lying " 'round about, deep and crisp and even," prove how inseparable Christmas and snow are. And this despite the fact that Jesus was born in one of the hottest climes in the world!

Narske Julekage

Cardamom is the delicate spice which gives this Norwegian Christmas cake its distinctive flavor. Even if you have never made a yeast bread before, don't be afraid to try—it is quite simple, and the taste of this wonderful fruit bread will make your family want this as their traditional Christmas

Yields: Two loaves

2 envelopes active dry yeast
¼ cup warm water (105° to 115°F)
1 cup milk, scalded
¾ cup sugar
½ cup butter (1 stick)
1 teaspoon salt
1 teaspoon cardamom
2 eggs, lightly beaten
1 teaspoon grated lemon peel
½ cup currants or golden raisins
½ cup mixed candied fruits, chopped
½ cup citron, chopped
¼ cup candied orange peel, chopped
½ cup nutmeats, chopped or broken
5 cups all-purpose flour
1 cup all-purpose flour, reserved

Two lightly-greased loaf pans,
8½" × 3½" × 2½"

Dissolve the yeast in warm water. If it is active, it will bubble. If it doesn't, try a fresh package. Heat the milk to just below boiling, and in a large mixing bowl, pour it over the sugar and butter. Let the melted mixture cool to lukewarm. Beat in the yeast, salt, cardamom, eggs, grated lemon peel and candied fruits and nutmeats. Beat in five cups of the flour, and if the dough is fairly stiff, you will not need the reserved cup of flour. Turn the dough out on a floured board and knead for eight to 10 minutes, until the dough is elastic and smooth. Roll the dough ball around in a lightly buttered bowl to coat the surface, then cover the bowl tightly with plastic wrap or a towel. Place in a warm spot (80° to 85°F) for about an hour, so that the dough may rise and double in bulk. Punch down and knead three or four times to get out the yeasty gas bubbles. Shape the dough into two loaves—either oblong for the loaf pans, or rounds for 9" cake pans—and place in lightly greased baking pans. Cover and let rise again until doubled in bulk. This second rising takes about 40 minutes. [*Preheat oven to 350°F.*] Bake the long loaves for 40 to 45 minutes (round loaves 30 to 35 minutes), or until done. Test for doneness after 35 minutes (in case your oven or your altitude has baked them more quickly) by taking a loaf out of the pan and tapping the bottom. A hollow sound means it is done. Let cool in the pan for a few minutes, then turn out on a rack to cool.

St. Lucia's Buns

Yields: 20 buns

2 envelopes active dry yeast
½ cup lukewarm water
1 pinch sugar
¾ cup milk, scalded
⅓ cup sugar
1 teaspoon salt
¼ cup butter
1/16 teaspoon powdered saffron (optional)

1 egg plus 1 egg yolk
2 ½ cups all-purpose flour
1 cup all-purpose flour, reserved
¼ cup golden raisins
1 egg white, lightly beaten
¼ cup blanched almonds, finely chopped
2 tablespoons sugar

Two lightly greased baking sheets

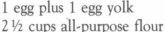

Stir the yeast into the warm water and add a pinch of sugar to proof. In a large mixing bowl, pour the scalding hot milk over the sugar, salt, butter and saffron, stir, and allow to cool. Stir in the yeast, eggs and 2½ cups of the flour, and beat the batter with a large spoon until it is smooth. Add enough of the remaining cup of flour to make a soft dough. Turn out on a lightly floured surface and knead for eight to 10 minutes, until smooth and elastic. Roll the dough ball around in a lightly buttered bowl to coat the surface, cover the bowl and let rise in a warm place (80° to 85°F) for about 75 to 90 minutes until doubled in bulk. Turn the dough out, and let rest for a few minutes before dividing. Cut dough into 20 pieces and roll each into a long strip about as big around as your finger and nearly 12″ long. Take one end in each hand, and coil the ends back to the center. For traditional buns you may bend the two coils back to back to make a single bun; or you may bake them as is for flat buns. Place on greased baking sheets, cover with waxed paper, and let rise until doubled in bulk—about 30 minutes. [*Preheat oven to 375°F.*] Press one or two raisins in the center of each coil before brushing the buns with the beaten egg white. Sprinkle with a mixture of almonds and sugar and bake for 15 or 20 minutes, or until golden. Cool on racks.

Kissing Balls

There are only two musts for a proper kissing ball. First it must have a sprig of mistletoe attached to the bottom of it, and it must be hung so that two people can kiss under it! The ball may be made from, and decorated with, practically anything. A large round potato or a ball of styrofoam works best. The idea is to have a firm base into which all kinds of things can be pinned, poked or stuck so as to completely cover the base.

One style is to cover a raw potato with natural things like holly, boxwood, small pinecones, seedpods and mistletoe. The moisture in the potato will keep the greens fresh for several days. Bore a hole through the potato and string it with a knotted cord or, say, a plaid nylon ribbon (which won't rot). Cut everything to approximately the same length (about three inches)—the twigs of boxwood and holly, etc.—and, if necessary, attach wire to the pinecones. Sharpen ends of twigs and stick everything into the potato, covering it with a dense "wig" of greenery. The mistletoe should be stuck in the bottom. If fresh mistletoe is hard for you to find, you might use an artificial sprig. The real berries are poisonous to animals, and perhaps the artificial would make you feel safer. As a final touch, if desired, add small narrow bows of ribbon glued to wooden toothpicks.

Another style, which can result in an even more individualistic kissing ball, utilizes cloth, ribbons, sequins or pearls, in fact anything at all. This style works best with a styrofoam ball, particularly if you want to cover the ball with fabric—say a plaid taffeta or velvet. Use glass-headed pins or hatpins to stick everything on. Some styrofoam seems more dense than others—perhaps short straight pins will work perfectly well. A formal ball might have velvet, taffeta ribbon, pearls and lace. A country ball might have calico or gingham, rick rack, small artificial cherries and pinecones.

Because kissing balls are so much fun to make, why not have everyone in the family who wants to make one sit around the kitchen table a week before Christmas, sharing odd materials and techniques. If all of you do styrofoam balls, in a few years you will have kissing going on all over the house!

Some New Traditions to Start

 Take a group photograph of everyone—one on Christmas morning, just outside the front door (you'll get the weather and the wreath with this one), and another sometime later in the day, perhaps at the table just as dinner begins. The grouping and even the poses can be the same every year, and a wonderful collection of pictures will result.

Encourage everyone in the clan to wear something red and something green. You will be surprised at how festive this can look! Children, especially, will get into the spirit of mixing two of their favorite bright colors.

 Decorate a very large cardboard carton (or buy a huge laundry basket which you can keep year after year) to hold the crumpled tissue paper, ripped wrapping paper, cord and mailing boxes from unwrapped presents. When the box or basket is full, and all the presents are unwrapped, see if your family dog or cat will sit in the box, with a ribbon around its neck, for a Christmas picture!

Make an Advent picture gallery. Buy a colored piece of posterboard from an art supply store, and draw picture frames on it, row after row, with a felt pen. Make enough for all the days of Advent—count days starting the fourth Sunday before Christmas Eve. Take an instant picture each day, or mix photos with pictures from your newspaper. Cut to fit and glue the corners to the cardboard. Write a short explanation of each picture, and what it means to your family, underneath.

Call two faraway friends or relatives to wish them a Merry Christmas. Long distance doesn't cost very much, and a five-minute phone call will bring you close and spread the good cheer of the season.

Make a manger scene that you can add to each year. The figures can be made of clay, like the ones on pages 38 and 39, carved from wood (balsa wood is very easy to cut and paint), made from cut-out paper with easel backs, twisted from wire and wrapped in yarn or cloth, or created by painting and re-dressing inexpensive dimestore toys. The Moravians of Pennsylvania, Virginia and North Carolina are famed for their *putz.* These are elaborate scenes not only of the manger in Bethlehem, but of all the surrounding community—the hills, the town, even the desert across which the Three Wise Men journeyed. The *putz* are brought out each year and set up, sometimes filling the end of a room. If you have small children or pets, this might be too ambitious and dangerous, but you could create a scene on a shelf of a cupboard in the dining room, or a table top in the living room.

 Buy funny little presents to use as table favors for everybody at Christmas dinner. Wrap them elaborately, and enjoy the shared laughter of your family.

 Every year make a wreath of cloth, ribbon, dried pinecones, artificial fruit, colorful beads and buttons, or a collage of Christmas cards, and after several years you will have a permanent wreath to hang on every door in the house.

A Gallery of Christmas Photographs

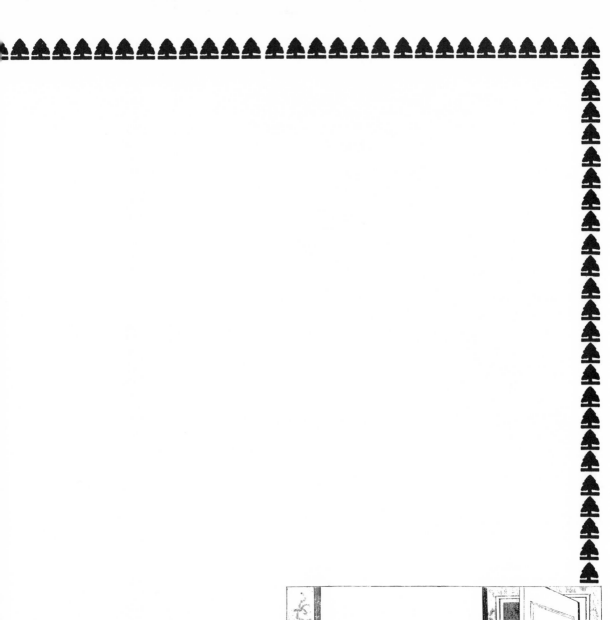

More Christmas Pictures

A Christmas Service
CELEBRATING THE BIRTH OF CHRIST

Date _____ Time _____ Hymns _____

Where was the service held? _____

Who officiated? _____

Readings _____

Title of Sermon _____

Notes _____

Christmas Cards

A Christmas Card

"I will send you a Christmas card," she said
When I bade her goodbye that night at the ball,
And she blushed, I am sure, as she softly spoke—
'Twas among the flowers at the end of the hall,
And it may be the shade of a crimson rose
Which splendidly grew near her perfect face,
Lent part of its hue—yet still, I think
She blushed, as she dropped those words of grace.

We had finished a valse, and Lander's men
Were strumming a rapturous serenade
As we slowly strolled by the palms and ferns,
Till we stopped where a fountain gently played.
I had told of my sudden, hurried start,
Her mien was so kind that my hopes rose high—
But Jack Steyne came up—'twas his dance he said;
So she left me then with that soft good-bye.

And this is the Christmas card she has sent;
The card that I've counted the hours to greet,
The card that I've fancied her pausing to choose
With tender blushes and veiled eyes sweet.
Oh, well, I am glad, on the whole, looking back,
That Steyne dropped in that night at the ball,
For this Christmas card is of bridal white,
And Jack's name is on it with hers—that's all.

From "The New-York Times," December 23, 1894

More Special Cards We Received

Displaying Christmas Cards

Gone are the days when people received hundreds of Christmas cards—the days when postage, and cards, were less expensive. But even 25 or 50 cards can pose something of a display problem. One of the most attractive solutions is shown here. It makes it possible to see and reread all the cards, and add to the holiday decorations at the same time.

First measure the height of the windows in the room(s) where you want to show the cards. Or, if you have lots of cards, measure the length of the draperies or curtains. Buy lengths of two- or three-inch wide ribbon, upholstery trim or similar yardgoods, or use handwoven Mexican or Guatemalan sash belts. You can even make your own from colored felt—perhaps with simple cut-outs of holly and bells spaced every 6″ so that they will show between the cards.

Use a ribbon on both sides of each window. Pin the cards to the ribbons with straight pins, spacing them evenly and not too far apart. If you wait until just two or three days before Christmas, most of your cards will have been received, and read, by the family, and it is easier on the arms to pin the cards on before hanging the ribbon up. Pin one end of the ribbon to the top of the drapery, and add a simple ribbon bow of the same or contrasting color at the top, to give it a finished look. The same idea can be adapted on either side of an archway into the living room, or for the banisters of a stairway in the hall. If carefully applied and removed, double-sided tape will hold the be-carded ribbons and will not pull off paint or varnish.

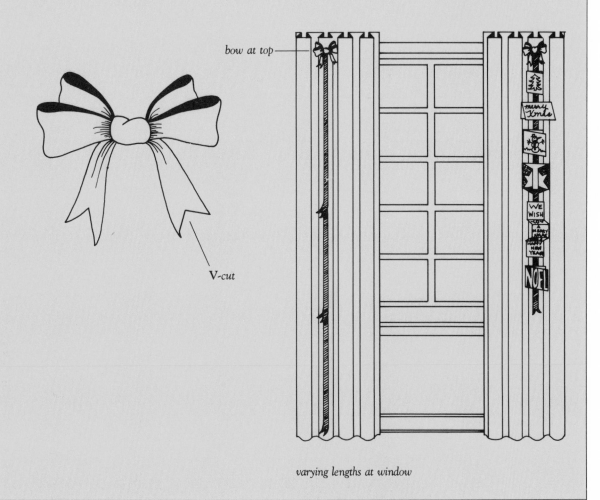

bow at top

V-cut

varying lengths at window

The Cards We Sent

Our Christmas Card List

If you wish to transfer addresses and phone numbers from your address book, please do. Otherwise, fill in just the names. Write addresses and numbers in pencil so that they may easily be updated.

Name	Address	Sent a Card	Wrote Letter	Telephoned	Card Returned
1					
2					
3					
4					
5					
6					
7					
8					
9					
10					
11					
12					
13					
14					

Name	Address	Sent a Card	Wrote Letter	Telephoned	Card Returned
15					
16					
17					
18					
19					
20					
21					
22					
23					
24					
25					
26					
27					
28					
29					
30					
31					
32					
33					
34					

Name	Address	Sent a Card	Wrote Letter	Telephoned	Card Returned
35					
36					
37					
38					
39					
40					
41					
42					
43					
44					
45					
46					
47					
48					
49					
50					
51					
52					
53					
54					

Index